LEAD GENERATION FOR REAL ESTATE AGENTS

(2nd Edition)

By

Greg Reed

Copyright

PRELUDE

In the early part of my real estate career I would sit patiently in my office waiting for my next sale to walk in. Well 'next' might be exaggerating it a little. '<u>A</u>' sale would be more appropriate.

Each night I'd return home and let out a bunch of expletives that would make my dog blush. I was often in a foul mood.

Then after 10 years of struggle I discovered, developed and implemented a bunch of real estate marketing strategies which I revealed in the first edition of this book, that saw my income virtually double in one year. After 2 years of using those real estate lead generation skills my income shot up another 50%. Add another 10 years and the lead generation business is in a whole new world.

The word soon got out that I had discovered a way to make 'easy' (no such thing) real estate sales. Real estate referrals became my method of operation.

Companies were approaching me to move camps. In fact, one company placed me on a $200,000 package to help boost sales. The strategies worked for me and they'll work for you.

This book is for real estate sales people, real estate agents or brokers who are totally overwhelmed with the complexities of selling real estate. It's for agents seething with frustration at their pathetic sales. And it's also for successful real estate agents wanting to take their real estate career to the next level.

You have two obstacles from making a killing in real estate sales:

1. You have no idea what business you are REALLY in. Most real estate sales people think that they are in the real estate business to assist people with their real estate buying, selling, leasing or managing needs. While partly 'true' unless you have a real estate lead that wants to buy, sell, lease or manage a property through you, you have no business. PERIOD.

2. A belief that you are 'Gods' answer to all things real estate. Let's face it. Real estate agents are an egotistical bunch. I can say that as I was a selling agent for 20+ years.

How often do you see advertisements stating "Billy Blogs – No. 1 For XYZ Real Estate" or "Cheryl Champion – Top Real Estate Marketer, Mars Tribune"

Who gives a toss?

The public certainly don't and nor should you, especially if you are a newbie just getting started. With my real estate lead generation tips, you'll soon be the 'king' or queen' of your local area.

My real estate lead generation strategies are by no means complete. But they are a good start in raising you from the depths of despair to making you the champion agent you so rightly deserve to be.

Here's my appeal to you. Believe in yourself. Believe in your real estate career.

Follow my suggestions. Implement those that resonate with you and be consistent.

These real estate lead generation strategies take time but they have helped me sell over $400 million of real estate. They will work for you too.

INTRODUCTION

I decided to write this book out of pure frustration. Frustration both on my part and for many real estate agents. Over the years I have asked many real estate sales people this question.

"What type of business are you in?"

You can imagine the looks I get especially when I'm the guy standing at the front of the room who is supposed to know what he is talking about.

Most agents fire back at me at rapid speed with something like:

"We are in the real estate business" or
"We help people buy and sell houses"

or the from the entrepreneurial types
"We help people become wealthy"

Heebie Jeebies! give me strength. While all of the above suggestions are true to some extent (yes even for those toe tapping, back slapping, high 5ing wealth creation masters) the REAL business real estate agents are in is:

REAL ESTATE LEAD GENERATION

Yep lead generation. Without having somebody to talk to whether they are a buyer or seller, business does not move forward. And we all know what happens to a business that becomes stagnant. It falls behind and eventually goes out of business.

So, to be successful in real estate you must become a lead generating machine! A real estate lead generation jedi!

When I discovered this the light bulb went on as if it was New Year's Eve 1999! Night seemed like day. It was that bright!

My career changed virtually overnight. How did becoming a lead generation master help me?

Here's a little about me and why I can confidently talk about generating leads.

"The satisfaction of helping a buyer/seller achieve a positive result. That's what makes me tick. It energizes me every single day. In my 20+ year real estate career I've sold over 700 properties and each and every sale has been a personal reward in itself. When I'm entrusted with the responsibility of selling someone's home, I'm driven by the knowledge that my mission is to find the perfect seller/buyer match.

I love the flexibility and variation of real estate; every home and every apartment are unique. My role is to help sellers find suitable buyers for their never-ending myriad of designs in equally diverse locations.

When I'm not working in real estate, I treasure my time with my family particularly the simple pleasures of a meal together or just catching up on everybody's day. Above all, it's vitally important to me that I'm a great husband and role model for my children.

People say I'm result orientated, tenacious and that I'm client focused. I'm perfectly comfortable with that. Selling your home is a big decision and it's one that I take very seriously indeed

I look forward to being able to help you in the upcoming sale of your home."

IT'S TRUE! GREG SOLD 11 HOMES IN JUST 5 HOURS!

Give Greg Reed a challenge and he'll deliver amazing results consistently. He is a man who knows real estate inside out and understands how to provide solutions for clients; clients who become passionate advocates of his services.

A vigorous combination of commitment, energy, focus, negotiation skills and a stringent code of ethics is needed to sell 11 homes in 5 hours. And that's what Greg achieved in the "Ultimate Auction at Sanctuary Cove" in 1992. A total of $30million of real estate was sold in one day to delighted buyers by ecstatic sellers. It was a culmination of countless hours that ensured a successful day was had by all.

The focus Greg harnessed to achieve this result continues into every property transaction he is involved with today. Sellers who have been involved with Greg attest to his energy, passion and enthusiasm. And above all his determination to deliver the best possible outcome for his clients is paramount.

This relaxed, outgoing professional has been responsible for personal sales in excess of $400 million in his real estate career; an industry he is very passionate about.

In a "prior" lifetime Greg has been a highly successful Fleet Sales Manager and Consultant within the tough, competitive motor industry (recognized amongst the Best 20 in Queensland for 2 years running) and a member of Mirvac's elite Investor Services team producing over 50+ sales in just 5 months.

Ask his clients why Greg is so successful and time after time they reply "He is a fantastic listener. He genuinely takes the time to listen to you and then relentlessly goes about his task to achieve the best possible results for you. He's great."

Real estate has its very own ecosystem. You need to know how everything fits together in order to maximize your returns.

Things began to change after wading through the pool of 'financial sludge' for years, I discovered 3 words to build my strategies around:

ATTRACT ENGAGE CONVERT

1. Attract – people can't buy property from you if they don't know of you.
2. Engage – people buy from people they know, like and trust
3. Convert – people won't buy unless all their concerns are dealt with

These 3 words will help you plant your career firmly in the rich soil of property, nurture your career into tall, thick, unbreakable gum trees and reach for the sky of financial freedom.

As I said when I first started this book, my real estate sales career was initially like re-an-acting the death scene in Macbeth on a daily basis. I was selling one property a month.

But by developing and implementing the lead generation tips back then and the new 2020 editions I'm about to give you, I unlocked the concept behind the attract/engage/convert philosophy which ultimately opened the flood gates for me.

The skills that I reveal in the coming pages helped me sell over $400 million in real estate, including 11 homes in 5 hours and numerous sales months of 12 – 16 property sales. They work!

Finally, you must have some talent to carry out a sale. You must understand how to affect a sale, what to do, what to say.

Real estate lead generation strategies won't make sales for you. In fact, if you become good at generating leads but are a flop in making a sale, then you'll further frustrate an already sub-par career.

However, assuming you do fit the profile of a competent real estate sales person, have the tenacity to stick at something for long enough for it to work and realize everything in life takes WORK, let's get started.

In the next few chapters, you will become a real estate lead generating jedi!

TABLE OF CONTENTS

DEDICATION

This book is dedicated to all those real estate agents who are struggling in their real estate career.

Too many people join the real estate profession and are not given the proper training or tools to become great. For too long these people have blamed themselves for their dismal results. But you are not to blame.

You possibly entered the business and were taught nothing about real estate lead generation or prospecting because your boss didn't really know how to generate leads him or herself. The real estate industry is full of people not knowing what the business is REALLY about and trying to teach others how to do it. Crazy; isn't it?

Well no more. Your time has come to change all of that. It's your time to break the shackles of mediocrity and become a real estate giant.

Let the journey begin.

STRATEGY #1
The Omnipresence Method

I'm going to teach you a method that will produce your ideal client, buyer or seller, for around a dollar a day. Big promise I know but read on.

If you are sick to the back teeth of dropping a small fortune on real estate portal ads and banners hoping to get customers but ending up with zilch or ending up with over priced listings owned by tight fisted, ankle biting manic whiners, then this could be your answer.

You know who I'm referring too. The pain-in-the-butt buyers or sellers who either give you super low ball offers or demand over the top prices while insisting you pay for all the marketing and then accept a low commission rate. As Arnie said "Let's terminate them"

If you're still shaking your head in agreeance, you'll probably be feeling sick in the stomach every time

Facebook automatically deducts another 'gazillion dollars' off your credit card and still you have no decent leads.

What I'm about to show you at a fraction of the cost you are probably spending on advertising, will put you in front of 100 ideal customers a day.

I call it the <u>Omnipresence Method</u> and it was first introduced to me by my copywriting coach.

The Oxford dictionary defines Omnipresence as

omnipresence

/ˌɒmnɪˈprɛz(ə)ns/

Learn to pronounce

noun
1. the state of being widespread or constantly encountered.
"the omnipresence of the Internet in society today"
the presence of God everywhere at the same time.
"how does God's universal action prove His omnipresence?"

The part that I'm going to focus on here is "the state of being widespread". Being seen everywhere.

Think of Nike.

Every time you see the tick you know it's Nike. Nike

is everywhere. On shoes, clothing, billboards, sports stars – everywhere.

But don't worry. You won't need millions if not billions of dollars to implement this method of marketing yourself to generate leads. I'm about to show you the same concept at only $1/day.

WHAT DO YOU NEED TO GET STARTED?

- **A Facebook (or Instagram) Business page.**

  Not your personal profile. If you don't have one, go to your personal profile and click on the 'Create a Page' Tab. Complete by adding text and photos. You're good to go.

- **An Offer**

  This is not your latest house listing. It's more about <u>what you can do</u> for a client and the benefit to them.

  "Let me show you how to own 3 investments properties for only $59 per week"

  " Retire early using my property investment hack that'll put you on the beaches of Hawaii sipping cocktails"

4

Who is the offer for.

The answer is not………everybody.

You must be specific and then you must tailor the offer for that specific market.

You might therefore run several of these campaigns but you don't have to. Just don't run a broad campaign because you'll miss so many customers with specific needs.

Let's look at the offer examples above. Your target markets might be:

* Couples nearing retirement; no kids
* Couples nearing retirement; with kids
* Single men nearing retirement
* Single women nearing retirement

You would need different posts for each of these specific markets using different words and image

STEP #1 CREATE YOUR CONTENT

Create around 10 – 30 pieces of content using images and text, plain text and videos. Make this content educational, customer focused or offers and speak to your audience, not about you.

Here I've used a stick image to give you a basic idea. Your posts should have eye catching images

Educational Example

"Here's how to buy your first house"

STEP #2 UPLOAD YOUR POST TO YOUR FACEBOOK PAGE

Upload at least 14 days' worth of posts; up to 30 days. Ideally you should post 2 – 3 times a day but one is sufficient to get you started.

This I admit is a big task especially when you are trying to list and sell property.

I recommend 'cheating' a bit here. I use a scheduler for all my posts.

I simply load my posts for my page, set the day and time for them to appear and then allow them to appear over the week.

If I'm running a promotion, like launching a book, offering a discount on a product or service (you might discount professional photography for a seller by 50%) or just giveaway something (free programmatic marketing for a month), then I will repeat the post at set intervals say every four days. That means the post will be shown seven times during the month.

Some people may think that this might be too much but with dropping reach rates on all social media, I doubt whether my audience will even see the same post twice.

STEP #3 ANALYSISE POST ENGAGEMENT

With about 20 posts up, it's time to find out which posts are resonating with followers.

Jump onto your Page and click **Insights.** We want to see the winners.

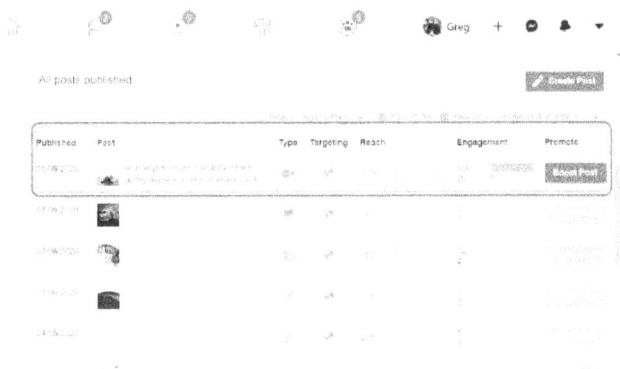

While two posts on this page got reasonable reach, the video at the top was seen by 2,700 viewers in just 5 days. Five hundred plus people engaged by liking, commenting or sharing this post.

This is clearly the winner and the post that should be further promoted.

For those of you on the run and not always at a desktop, grab the Facebook Page app from the Apple store or where you can download apps for android. Look out for the yellow flag symbol.

STEP #4 BOOST YOUR POST

Just hit the Boost Post button on the post, select your audience and budget, wait for Facebook's approval and you're set to go.

Now I know some of you 'advanced Facebook marketers will say that boosting a post is a waste of money. And if my aim for you here was to make sales, I'd agree.

But our main purpose is to get you seen everywhere. This builds familiarity. People get to know, like and trust you. Then you can focus on sales.

Imagine if you had three or five posts that organically

did well and for just a dollar a day for each, you and your brand was now in front of thousands of people for say $5/day.

What could happen in a month? Tens of thousands, possibly hundreds of thousands of fresh eyes discovering you and your real estate business. What do you think might happen to your sales? They'd go up, legend!

And before I finish this step, you're probably wondering about who makes up the audience for you to boost too?

That can be as simple as showing the post to people who like your page and their followers.

If you want to target say 35-55-year-old men who love fishing, boating and surfing, you can create an audience by selecting the target audience button and putting in your filters.

STEP #5 RINSINCE AND REPEAT

Repeat the popular posts. If your educational posts are getting more likes, comments and shares organically, do more of those.

If people are loving your customer focused videos of

new house owners standing in front of a sold sign or their house, shoot more of these.

Within a month or two you'll have sufficient data via your Insights to know what your followers love. Do what they love. It's the shortest path to your success!

Keep tweaking; keep refining. Boost engaged organic posts and repeat.

STRATEGY #2
Intent Based Branding

Frank Kern is a master marketer, probably one of the best direct response copywriters and now a modern-day guru using social media.

I've used this method several times before and seen spectacular results. Currently I'm doing Frank's 3.0 version of intent based branding and loving the outcome.

Here's my review on how Frank uses this method and why I 100% believe you should have this in your lead generation system.

WHAT IS INTENT BASED BRANDING?

"Producing assets that actually helps people, thereby building a relationship with cold prospects and finally converting them into sales"

Being a paid client of Frank's and undertaking his

latest Intent Based Marketing 3.0 thirty-day challenge; that's my interpretation.

<u>The big 'trick' here is to actually help somebody</u>. This would seem obvious but most agents tend to leave the big stuff out hoping to cash in later.

That's so 1980's garbage. It doesn't work anymore.

Customers want real information that will actually help them. Otherwise they'll flick off to another YouTube video or read another blog post that does provide the answer to their problem.

My suggestion is that you use the oldest trick in the book and actually help them.

WHAT DO YOU DO?

Let's look at intent based branding around getting sellers to auction their homes.

1. **Who - identify your market?**

   This is pretty simple. We are directing our marketing towards home owners.

2. **What problems do home owners face?**

   There are various types of owners who maybe wanting to sell their homes.

Home owners needing to relocate to another area.

Home owners under financial stress.

Home owners with a unique quality making it hard to value.

Home owners wanting a quick result at the best possible price.

3. **How can we help these various owners?**

We need to produce assets, in this case short videos, answering these problems for the owner.

For example, if we were targeting owners looking for a quick sale while maximizing their price, we might create videos around:

a. Preparing their home for sale – minor fix – ups, lawn maintenance, decluttering inside.

b. What local government documents should they have or need to get. Has there been any extensions to the home like an additional carport for which the owner will need to produce evidence showing the work has been approved?

c. What finance options are there to carry out marketing campaigns, do minor repairs to maximize the sale of the property.

d. How long does the marketing campaign need to run for?

HOW TO SELL STUFF?

Now that we've been helping home owners get their home ready for an auction and given them tips on maximizing the price, we need to introduce ourselves as the real estate agent who can best help them achieve the outcome they desire.

Giving free information over a few videos has endeared us to a protentional seller that we are a trustworthy agent to best help them. We've proved ourselves.

Most agents still go about this client getting process by talking to prospects in the language of an agent.

"I'm #1 in the office"

"The Boston Tribune has recognized me as the best marketer of real estate in the city"

"I did seven auctions last month"

Kudos for the agent who has such accolades but a real estate seller doesn't really care. They want to deal with somebody <u>who can show, not tell</u>, they are competent and get the job done.

Sellers also want to know that agents have their back. They want to feel that an agent will stand up for them, protect them and go the extra mile.

Producing four, five or six videos on how to prepare your home for auction will go a long way to building confidence in a seller that you are the best agent to look after them.

Your offer to do business is delivered in a very casual way.'; the softly, softly approach. The tone is confident but a little laid back. It's almost like a 'last minute throw in'. You kind of indicate that you don't mind if they do engage or not.

In sales terminology we would call this the take away. And here's the weird thing about take away closes. The more you are evasive, casual in your delivery the more somebody wants it!

WHAT TO SAY IN YOUR VIDEOS?

Here's a simple script to use in your video.

1. **The call out** – If you, do you.

   We want to identify immediately who the video is for. This is target marketing. We don't want people to watch the video if they are not our target.

   "If you are thinking of selling your home and want to do it in the shortest possible time and get the best price, listen up"

2. **Preview** – In this video, we're/I'm going to show you how to add an extra $10,000 value to the sale price just by de-cluttering your home........."

3. **Offer (soft)** – "If you want us to show you how you can get the best price for your home, head on over to our/my website and click on the Book A Call button.........."

4. **Content** – "So here's how you can add an extra $10,000 to your sale price.........make the house look bigger.....remove non-essential furniture..... replace oversized furniture with smaller pies,...... consider getting the home professionally staged... perhaps freshen up the internal paint work with light, neutral colours........"

5. **Offer** – "If you found this video helpful, why not book a call with us/me. We can....."

Imagine the response you'll get to this free type of marketing. You'll generate a ton of leads to keep your prospecting funnel full. The purpose of these videos is for a 'suspect' to become a prospect and enter your sales process.

It could be 'book a call', grab a free report on your

suburb or a downloadable pdf on how the auction process works.

An agency needs leads. Without a lead there can be no appraisal of a property. No listing, no sale and no commission. It all starts with a lead and intent based branding delivers cold leads in a warmer state.

Thanks Frank. If you want to upskill yourself, Frank Kern is a sensational coach. Join his private mentorship programs and skyrocket your marketing and career.

"Good video; all facts. No adjectives. All Specifics. Sold a lot of real estate"

David Ogilvy (adapted for real estate)

STRATEGY #3
Rank on Google With No Money

We all know that ranking well on Google will drive traffic to your website and ultimately increase your chances of getting leads.

Achieving this result usually takes money, sometimes lots of money through Google paid ads.

But there is a way to get onto the front page of Google for your keyword (words or phrases people use to search to find things) without spending money.

3 WAYS TO GET RANKED ON GOOGLE

1. ROUND UP POSTS

a. **Blog**

The first thing you'll need is a website with the ability to create blog posts. Wordpress is the easiest way to do this. If you have difficulties with this get your web designer to set this up, watch a tutorial on YouTube or go to Fiverr.com and type in "set up a Wordpress blog into the search box. You'll find hundreds of people from around the world who can help you, starting at just $5.

b. **Google experts** or top performers in the keyword that you want to write about. Let's use kitchen renovations for this example.

In addition to any ads that appear on the first page for this keyword, you should see ten companies or experts in the kitchen renovation industry.

c. **Approach** each of these companies by saying something like:

"Hey John

I've seen lots of good articles and reviews about your kitchen renovations. You're definitely the expert in this field and I'm a big fan.

I'm putting together an expert guide to kitchen renovations in Sydney for my real estate blog and I'd love to include you as one of the best kitchen renovators in that post.

Can I arrange a time to ask you a few questions………….."

d. **Gather all the opinions**.

Create the post and link back to all the experts you've quoted. Include a thumbnail image of the person you spoke to and their business logo in the post.

Ask them to share the post on their social media platforms and website.

They may even give you a link back to your website. Google loves link backs.

Using this method gets your post shared for free. The more shares, the more authority you gain not only on social media but also Google. Your site gets more traffic and you move up the Google ranking ladder.

What other topics can you think of?

'The best lawn care for Spring in Chicago'

'The best exterior paint to weather your beachside house in Palm Beach'

2. UBERSUGGEST KEYWORD DENSITY TOOL

Type in your competitors url/domain name. eg https://raywhite.com

Scroll down the page and discover all the SEO keywords that business is ranking for.

These keywords describe to Google what the business is about.

However this doesn't mean that you grab all their keywords and shove them into your blog posts or website. Keyword stuffing isn't liked by Google and you'll be penalized with poor rankings.

Instead what it is saying to Google is that their site is more thorough in providing valuable information on a topic and Google is rewarding them by pushing them up the rankings. This is helping them get more leads and that's what you want.

Therefore you must be more thorough with your posts. You must go deep with your answer so that your post truly helps somebody.

Check out your competitors keywords that are do well and do a more thorough job.

If they rank for '14 Ways to Sell Your House Faster in Cairns' in a 500 word post, you give the enquiring public '25 ways……..' in a 1,000 – 1,5000 word post.

3. **WRITE APPEALING POST – COPY ADS**

Go to Ubersuggest.com and type in a broad keyword. Let's use home buying. That keyword attracts 33,100 searches per month in the US.

That's good but also relatively difficult to rank for because you'd be competing with a lot of big companies like real estate franchises, real estate portals, banks, insurance companies and a like.

Instead look for long tail keyword phrases. These by definition have a number or words in them but are still popular.

The keyword phrase 'home buying with bad credit' has 2,900 searches per month and is easier to rank for.

Rather than trying to rank for 'home buying in New York' the phrase 'First home buyer in New York' has a healthy 3,600 searches every month.

Now that you have your keyword phrase check out the ads on Google on that phrase and look for eye catching headlines. Google reward great headlines and of course somebody's ad spend.

Instead of "Buying your first home in New York" (which is ok), punch it up with "Funky New York Pads For First Home Buyers That Won't Break The Bank"

FINAL TIPS

Use the keyword in your meta-tag description (Google that term or watch a YouTube video).

Use a date in your title eg 'Gardening Tips for Spring 2021'

Use words like, New, Fast, Get, Try, to increase your clicks.

[[SUCCESS STORY]] First National Hills Direct

First National Hills Direct is an award-winning real estate office located in NSW for the First National Network.

Competition within the area is rife. Getting found on Google is a priority in getting organic search but there is a lot of competition from other agents.

The owners undertook a blogging program whereby they had four professionally written articles delivered into the inbox monthly.

Within a couple of months not only did the agency move up the Google rankings on page one, they also achieved a number of top four rankings for relevant keywords within the area; with some hitting #1.

STRATEGY #4
Become A Virtual Event Megastar

At the time of writing this book the world is in the grips of COVID-19, bludgeoned to within an inch of its life. Hundreds of thousands of people have died and the business world is in lock down.

At this time one of the only way's businesses can connect with customers is via virtual means; webinars, although they've been around for a while, they are now the talk of the town.

<u>Webinars are good but can be lack luster. To generate leads, we want brilliance!</u>

Because they are so mainstream now, not only are they losing their shine, but some people are screaming webinar fatigue and starting to switch off. And that's a pity because webinars are a great source for lead generation.

So how do we get around that? We pimp our webinars up. We create virtual EVENTS!

These events will be great for networking, will show you off us as an authority and help you become the dominator in your area,

Are you ready superstar? Buckle up!

VIRTUAL EVENTS DOMINATOR

1. **Create your event and include your social media links**

   When somebody registers for your event they get an automatic reply confirming their attendance and sharing all the necessary information about the upcoming webinar (ooops no wrong dowdy word), I mean event.

   This is perfect real estate for you to personalize the message. Sure, the event time, date and link are important but why not add your social media links like Facebook, Instagram or Twitter. Yes people still use Twitter; it's not reserved for Donald Trump tweets only.

2. **Promote your speakers**

   Dull boring webinars have only one speaker; that would be you. You're probably worth top billing but if you can attract a couple of speakers, it just takes the event to another level.

Grab their bio in advance, along with their picture and promote it all over social media.

Ask them to do the same.

Imagine if you can snare a 'big time' speaker? Sharing this to your Facebook page, dropping out a couple of tweets and throwing in a few boosted ads can really give your event the WOW factor.

Make your speakers the stars of the show and promote them as much as the event. Get the speaker to do some posts or tweets leading up to the event whereby viewers can ask questions.

The answers they give can be a great way to steer the event so people engage. Mention a question and the person who submitted it will be hooked for life.

3. **Add a Twitter feed to the event**

An Australian television show does this very well. Insight on the ABC, has a twitter feed and they attract a lot of comments. You can watch the show and tweet at the same time. Brilliant! Engaging! I'm hooked!

Every webinar/event platform has an in-built chat box. They work to some extent but people tend to ask boring questions like 'will there be slides after' or 'are you recording this'.

By using a hashtag, Twitter can pick up the conversation and allow your guests to focus on the event and drop questions in via Twitter. It also gives them the option to remain out of the spotlight.

4. **Create an event hashtag**

As mentioned above, it's a good idea to have an event specific hashtag.

Promote the hashtag to those who register, attendees and throughout your social media posts; especially on Twitter.

5. **Promote your event on LinkedIn**

I'm hoping that you do have a LinkedIn profile (more on that in a coming chapter) as it is the fastest growing business social media platform in 2020.

Facebook, Instagram and even Twitter may be great for likes and comments telling you how great you are, but LinkedIn will stamp you as an authority in your business niche.

I'll delve much deeper into this lead generating muscle machine later including how to set up your profile for maximum success along with a very sneaky hack that'll make you the champion in any niche.

Want to be the lifestyle real estate agent in Tampa, Florida? Hang on; it's coming! But for now, let's continue to set you up as the Event Queen or King.

6. **Pimp your event's chat pod.**

Don't be a bore. "Hi, I'm Greg. I'm an agent with XYZ Realty". Nope that's garbage.

How about "Hi, I'm Greg and I'm so excited to be here because today my very special guests are going to reveal how to shave 12 years off your mortgage without paying higher repayments"

Introduce the hashtag and ask everybody to share it. Get them to put it into their Twitter tweets so you can pick up their conversation.

7. **Are you a member of Meet-Ups?**

Meet-ups are a great way to network with like minded souls. If the group is unable to meet because of gathering restrictions, ask the host if you can advertise within the group and get them to log into your virtual event.

8. **Give away the event notes**

   Create some event notes and give them away after the event to those who attend. I'm strict on these though. I only give them to those who <u>attend</u>.

   People who register but fail to show up, won't read the notes in my opinion. Reward those who reward you with their attendance.

Events pimp up standard webinars. Pick the right speakers, promote the hell out of them, create and event hashtag and you'll have a virtual function that'll be the envy of the 'interwebs', knock your competitors for six, open the lead generation flood gate and make you the dominant authority in your industry ………..maybe even the world!

Dynamic LinkedIn Profile

A lot of people think of LinkedIn as a place to list your job profile. And they are partly right but they are missing the really big picture.

If you are involved in B2B sales, LinkedIn is the platform for you to focus on. It's on steroids!

Check it out these stats:

1. 675 million monthly users
2. 57% of users are men; 43% are women.
3. 30 million companies are on LinkedIn
4. 27% of US residents use LinkedIn
5. 70% of visitors come from outside the US. 11 million are in Australia.
6. 61% of users are aged 25 – 34 years
7. 57% of LinkedIn's traffic is mobile
8. 4 out of 5 people on LinkedIn are the decision makers in a company
9. An ad on LinkedIn reaches 12% of the world's

population

10. 94% of B2B marketers use LinkedIn for content creation

[Source: Hootsuite 2020]

LinkedIn is much more than a job posting site. If you want to generate great real estate leads, re-read those stats again but highlight #10 – content creation. This is where the lead generation magic occurs.

But before you can become a jedi with LinkedIn articles or posts, you'll need to create the best profile possible. We want you to be the 'attraction' real estate agent that CEO's of Fortune 500 companies rush to buy or sell their next waterfront mansion.

Procurement managers, general managers and logistic specialists within a company are making decisions daily about where their company's new headquarters or warehousing facility needs to be. You need to be top of mind when they need to make a move.

Let's get your profile right, right for 2020 and beyond.

PROFILE

1. **Profile picture**

   Use a professionally photographed picture in business attire. I'm not sure that real estate agents in Hawaii wear Hawaiian shirts and sip margaritas while selling real estate; I suggest you don't use your last vacation picture either.

2. **Use a professional background cover image**

   It should be around 1584 x 396 pixels. Canva.com is a great place to create your image

3. **Create a headline that draws eye balls to your profile**

   Titles are fine but don't always tell people exactly what you do. More importantly they don't tell people what you can do for them.

   Make the headline a message. Don't confuse people. If they have to use to many brain cells to decipher your message, they'll leave

   "I'm a property connector with people who are searching for their ideal abode that gives them inner peace" OR

"I sell real estate in New Farm"

4. **Write your own story**

The summary section is your first connection with a possible customer. Make it flow like a story.

5. **Speak to your audience**

Show people what you can do for them.

Words like 'focused, strategic thinker, global entrepreneur, thought leader and so on sound impressive, to you.

If I was engaging you to do some work for me I'd hope that you were focused, had a thought and were strategic. Drop the hype!

6. **Show off your skills**

Let people know exactly what you're good at without the fluff.

Use your skills as a heading and list companies you've worked for under that skill. To do this you simply sway the company name for the skill went creating your job experiences.

Warehouse Sales Consultant

Reed Properties

2007 -

Greg Garages

2002 – 2007

OR

Prestige Resort Broker

Sanctuary Cove
1999 -2002

Washington Golf Resort

1996 – 1999

Palm Lake Resort Nevada

1990 - 1996

This clearly identifies your skills to people wanting to engage a warehouse sales or prestige resort sale person in these examples.

7. **Get endorsements**

The easiest way to do this is to endorse others.

8. **Build your recommendation bank**

Send connections a link asking them to recommend you for a particular skill.

The best time to do this is right after you've done something great for them.

9. **Use the publication section on your profile**

If the publication section does not appear, go to Add Section in the right task bar and scroll down until you find it.

Click on it and update with any publications you've appeared in

Now that you have a decent profile, good images and you've uploaded some publications that you've appeared in, let's start working LinkedIn to generate more leads.

LEAD GENERATION ON LINKEDIN

Here's 9 ways to get more business

1. **Create a company page**

   Different than the standard profile. If you own a business, promote it on LinkedIn. It's the business resource where connected people hang out.

   Did you know that countries like the US, Australia or even Canada are wide open for building connections. They don't even rank in the Top 5 countries for average number of connections per user.

   When you set up your company page and upload your logo, you'll notice back on your personal profile this logo will also appear. This gives some legitimacy about the business and makes your profile more eye catching.

2. Post good quality, useful content

People on LinkedIn prefer to read good business type content. They have no interest in your cat photos.

LinkedIn gives you a number of options when posting. Write an article, upload a photo or video.

Make your articles the best you can. You are competing with 100,000 new articles a week. Do it right and your authority will soar.

Aim for 5 – 10 articles or uploads a week.

3. Search for individuals

Use the filter to search via location, company or connections. Connecting directly with an individual is the best way into a company you wish to do business with.

But there's an art to it. DON'T just hit the connect button with an individual. It doesn't make them feel special and it spotlights you as somebody who sees them as a number.

Instead of hitting the connect button, click on the More button and hit the personal invite button.

Complete a personal invite using their name and hit send.

Remember we live in a mobile world. Keep you invite message short but inviting. Make it standout and never try to sell in this invite.

I keep a standard invite within my notes on my phone. When I come across somebody I wish to connect with, I copy and paste the invite from my notes into the personal invite and hit send.

It's short, quick and easy for when I'm one the run.

I also have some standard follow ups within my notes as well.

4. **Leverage groups**

Join groups of interest or where you see potential business.

Be helpful. Don't sell. Be consistent.

Soon you'll be recognized as a helpful person worthy of a direct approach to do business with, rather than a pesty sales person that should be avoided.

5. **Start your own group**

   <u>This is where the power is. It's your group. You set the rules.</u>

   The big benefit is that you have the potential to build another database of contacts that you can build a relationship with that potentially may lead to more business.

   Be mindful of the general rule even it's your own group – post good quality content that helps the group members and don't always be selling.

6. **Follow the LinkedIn marketing blog**

   It is a great source of knowledge in growing your business.

   Be a regular commenter on posts. Your visibility will attract the right connections for you.

If you want to start generating hundreds of leads a week on LinkedIn, it can happen. But not overnight.

It'll take a ton of work posting good content daily over a long period of time.

By being consistent you'll blow 99% of your competitors out of the water.

You'll be the dominating real estate agent in your area.

STRATEGY #6
Create Blog Posts

If you want leads, you'll need to write blog posts.

But not any old blog post. In this chapter I break down what is essential to have in a blog post if you want to rank well in Google AND get a ton of real estate leads.

[Hint] Size matters.

THE BLOG POST STRATEGY OF WINNERS

Consistency also matters. Your blog posts need to be at least weekly to gain traction with the search engines.

1. **Let's dissect a good blog post**. You'll need

   A great headline

   Responsible for 80% of your blog being read. Be creative; not boring. Magazines have great headlines – study them.

Use an eye-catching image

Literarily suck the eye balls out of somebody. Get them to wrench their neck around fast, but not injure themselves.

Provide an introduction

It doesn't have to be long but it must be enticing. It must force the reader to want more.

Lead into the article

Outline the main points you'll cover in the article.

Main body

Write short sentences using easy, simple language. Most articles today are read on mobile devices. Your articles must be easy to read. Shorter paragraphs of only 3 lines are preferred.

Use sub-headings to grab a reader's attention.

Conclusion

Summarize all the points your outlined in your article.

Ask a question and seek feedback

Make your posts more engaging by asking a question at the end and seek comments.

"Which one of the above points above will you be implementing this month. Leave a comment and let's know."

2. Improve your SEO with the right keywords

Us a free tool like Ubersuggest.com to do your research on the best keywords and keyword phrase to use.

Start with words that have decent search enquiries but are not super competitive. Let the big boys go after those expensive terms.

Localize your search by adding your suburb or town onto the mix.

3. Create blog posts that scream value

Give the reading public what THEY want. Speak their language.

Answer questions. eg "What deposit is required to buy a house?"

Discuss problems eg "How to get more people to your open home?"

Discuss cost eg "What does it cost to auction my house?"

Do comparisons eg "Are fixed home loans better than variable interest loads?"

Create a list post eg "15 ways to sell your house quicker this winter"

Spotlight some reviews eg "The best real estate marketing tactics reviewed"

4. Use the AIDA formula for writing posts

AIDA stands for attention, interest, desire and action.

Check out this video for a great understanding and how to use AIDA

https://youtu.be/bvoxOtRq844

5. Get links to your posts

I've already discussed using keywords in your title, meta-description and body to create links.

Another strategy is to ensure you are also building external links with other companies and blogs. The higher the company's domain authority (DA) the stronger the link value.

You should aim to to build links via guest posting or commenting on sites with a DA 30 – 100. Amazon, Google, Youtube have DA 100.

Don't buy link building services from companies offering miracles. "Get 100,000 backlinks for $29".

The links are rubbish, most likely from sites with DA 1 and you'll hurt your chances to rank well with Google.

THE SECRET FORMULA TO DRIVE TRAFFIC TO YOUR BLOG

A guy who got 94 million visitors to his blog posts gave me this formula. I'm taking a punt he knows what he's talking about. Here's what he said.

Write response posts

Response posts are those that answer questions eg. "What are your management fees?"

Create ten of these articles first at 1000 words each.

Write stock posts

After you've finished writing your ten response posts, write ten stock posts. These need to be 2,000 – 2,5000 words and cover topics around 'how to' do something. List posts (using numbers) are also popular stock posts.

eg "How to declutter your house"
"7 ways to get a greener lawn this summer"

Write pillar posts

These are meaty posts. Usually they are 3,500+ words and cover the big topics and have all encompassing headlines like "The Definitive Guide To Selling Your House In Point Piper"

Be consistent, post weekly, follow these guidelines and use this strategy, and you'll start getting a flood of lead generating traffic to your website. Just give it time though. Blogging takes 6 – 12 months to see results.

[[SUCCESS STORY]] Marcus Sheridan – River Pools & Spas

Marcus owned River Pools and Spas up until 2017. In 2009 the GFC hit the US business economy hard including the pool selling business.

Marcus couldn't afford to continue to advertise his business. He was about to go broke.

Instead of waiting for the crash to swallow him up, he made things happened.

He started blogging…………………..about swimming pools. YES pools!

By 2011 traffic to his website had reached 87,000/month. In 2013 it was 300,000 visitors/month.

And when he sold the business in 2017, 600,000 visitors/ month.

Blog article writing works BUT only for those who do it consistently for a while.

STRATEGY #7
Email Marketing

For some, this title has already made you squirm. Screams of "Greg, are you mad?" can be heard for miles. Well not by me.

You might also be thinking that this strategy is so '1980's' and it doesn't work now.

And I get why you might be saying that.

But at the risk of turning you off, slamming this book closed or just moving onto the next chapter, let me say this to you. YOU'RE WRONG!

My conviction comes not from reading countless articles and books on the subject but actually doing it.

I can attribute millions of dollars in real estate sales to email marketing. I've created tons of leads with email and developed strong relationships with my lists.

A good percentage of my list members open my emails every week; around 38% on average. That's double the real estate industry standard!

I used the concepts behind email marketing (it was called fax marketing then) to sell 11 homes in just 5 hours for around $6,000,000. That was a great pay day!

But email marketing has not been a one hit wonder for me.

In the early 2000's I consistently sold 12 – 16 homes a month from my email list. Sixty-four homes in 5 months was pretty good going.

Today as a fiction author, my email list generally buys enough books at launch for my new book to rank in the Top 10 on Amazon US in category; sometimes hitting #1.

Do you think email marketing could help you generate leads and make sales? If so, let's read on.

EMAIL MARKETING IS ALIVE AND WELL

Here's more proof why email still works

According to Hubspot, 85% of the internet population are on email. That's around 6 billion people.

Email is more popular than search engine reach by around 15% and knocks out social media by 22%.

[[TIP]] Back a winner, start using email.

How do you get people onto your email list?

In exchange for somebody's email address you need to give away something for free. But not any old garbage. It must be something highly desirable and valuable.

It could be a free report like a suburb report, delivered monthly or quarterly.

A checklist on how to do something quickly could be of value to some people.

What about a video series on how to successfully bid at an auction without the bidder losing his/her shirt? That might be very desirable for some people.

Get permission to contact them

You might be giving away something for free to get people onto your list, but you'll also need their permission to keep on contacting them.

Without them agreeing to opt-in to your list or having the option to opt out, you might be in breach of the CAN SPAM Act, resulting in your ISP (internet service provider) banning you. Trying to get another provider to take you on once you are listed as a spammer will be almost impossible or at least very uncomfortable.

Give them great content

Provide great follow up content. <u>Really help people.</u>

Emails around:

- Should I pay for marketing?
- Should I go with a low-cost commission agent?
- What's better – auction or private treaty marketing

Would be interesting emails for list members to read.

These emails don't need to be long especially if you have a similar article on your website blog. Two to three hundred-word emails are plenty.

When to pitch?

The simple answer is when necessary.

You're not a benevolent society. The ultimate purpose of these emails is to make sales.

You need to add a pitch but not in every email. Do that and you'll get a massive unsubscribe rate. Do you hate being sold to all the time? So do your readers.

Start softly when trying to get commitments. Ask people to follow you on Facebook. Let them know you have a free webinar coming up next week. Invite them to ask a question.

Softly, softly wins the race. When you have a property to sell, they'll be more receptive.

Newsletters add great value (if done right)

The best newsletters mix business and personal messages well. Offer business messages like:

- Current listings
- Upcoming auctions
- Suburb or town developments
- Government updates

Along with personal messages:

- A personal story about your real estate career
- Spotlight a staff member eg "Introducing Sally our contract administrator"
- Celebrate a milestone eg "We've just turned 5" (add a nice picture of you and the team)
- Show some behind the scenes stuff eg "Here's Mike our photographer"
- Share a review eg "Peter has been fantastic throughout our selling process"
- Let readers into your personal life eg "On weekends, I'm a biker"

- Toss in an interview eg "Meet Jared our favourite barista. He'll be yours too)

Automate your emails

Write them once and set them free by using a scheduler. In email language that scheduler is referred to as an autoresponder.

With an autoresponder you write a series of emails to be sent at designated times.

These series include a welcome email, a download link to your free giveaway and a sequence of emails that leads your reader along a certain path; possibly to a sale.

Email campaigns can be general and work at building relationships. These general but informative email campaigns are critical to keep your name top of mind for when a prospect is ready to buy or sell again.

Some prospects are ready now and may have joined your email list because of an upcoming auction. An auction email campaign would provide details about the property, what to expect at the auction, what they need to do to prepare for the auction, what checks and balances they need to make like getting their finance approved or ordering a build and pest inspection prior to the auction day.

To discover what the best autoresponders are check out my comparison articles at:

https://emailedgar.com/getresponse-vs-active-campaign

https://emailedgar.com/getresponse-vs-mailchimp

Create specific lists

Not all readers need the same information. Emails about the auction process might not appeal to somebody who is trying to decide if your suburb is the right place for them to live.

Lists can easily be created around:

- Customers (those who have bought). They need information about the suburb/town, updates, ways to add value to their property. Your latest listing would not be of interest unless they are a serial investor.
- General newsletter subscribers eg listings would be included in these mailouts.
- Specific campaigns eg auction campaigns on a specific property.

Emails are known for giving a ROI of 44:1 in the online marketing world. That number may be difficult to determine for real estate transactions, but where agents commonly receive commissions of $10,000+ per sale, your ROI for sending a few automated emails, even over a year or two, would be well worth your while.

Facebook Live

Facebook is a goliath of opportunity for real estate agents to market themselves and their products.

There are plenty of other books on the market about Facebook marketing, so I've decided to leave organic posting via picture or text posts to those experts.

I'm also not a fan of Facebook general organic marketing as I've noticed over the years subscriber newsfeed reach is plummeting. In 2012 your newsfeed could be seen by about 15% of your subscribers when you posted your 'cat photos or foodie shots'. Now only 1-2% do.

In spite of Mr. Zuckerberg trying to pitch that he wants Facebook to return to its good old days of engaging with people via photo posts, this is simply fake news. Facebook is a public company with shareholders wanting a healthy return on their investment.

That means they demand profits. Profits come from

people buying stuff and in Facebook's case, that means advertisements.

Facebook ads are not all doom and gloom though and I'll look at them later as a means to generating real estate leads.

For now, though I'm going to persist with the organic approach to getting seen on Facebook with a strategy that'll give your branding a boost and generate leads on steroids; for free.

FACEBOOK LIVE – TIPS AND TRICKS TO CRUSH IT

Sixty six percent of viewers love Facebook Live. That's only second to Facebook itself who I assume love it 100%. I know one thing for sure, Facebook loves Live more than YouTube.

Live gives Facebook the opportunity for visitors to hang around more. YouTube takes them away and that's not desirable.

Here's how to make your Facebook Live videos zing, keep people on your page longer and have Facebook fall madly in love with you.

1. **Do a Q & A Session**

    People love getting answers to the questions they

ask. Sure they can read a post but video can be consumed quicker.

Live videos also show off your personality thereby attracting (hopefully not repelling) new customers.

If you want to maximize your Q & A audience, advertise your Live prior and do them on a specific day and time.

"Join me every Friday at 2pm when I answer all your real estate buying and selling questions LIVE!"

2. Teach Viewers Something

Generally these videos are slightly longer than your standard 2-minute session but they deliver a heap of value.

"In today's live video I'm going to show you how to makeover your bathroom in 5 minutes without spending a cent"

3. Interview Somebody Interesting

Have you got a real estate celebrity in your area? Why not interview them?

How about a local restauranteur? Video is great

for capturing passion and most chefs speak with great passion about their food.

Maybe you can offer a free dinner to a lucky viewer?

4. **Launch a New Product**

Is your company marketing properties using programmatic marketing (more on this later)?

Let the selling public know that you have this innovative marketing strategy where their home can be seen by 40,000 highly targeted people over a month.

This would be a great point of difference over your competitors who are seeking full page newspaper ad contributions to a platform that's dwindling in readership.

5. **Tour a Property Live**

Show off your latest listing with a Live tour.

These videos have a raw edge to them over professionally shot videos and keep viewers glued to the screen.

6. **Breaking News Announcement**

Interest rates just went up? Let your followers know about it via a Facebook Live video.

This has more punch than a Canva stock image.

7. Show Your Bloopers

Not all videos are perfect. Sometimes it takes many goes to get them right.

But don't edit the video or delete altogether because you've got a few umms and errs in there.

Keep rolling. People love the human side of videos.

8. Incorporate Your Brand

Here I mean YOUR brand. Your company has a brand usually depicted by a logo.

But Facebook Live gives you the opportunity to promote your own personal brand.

Do you drive a zippy vintage car to your open homes? Are you known for wearing scarves or single breasted linen jackets.

What ever it is, let your own style shine through the camera.

9. Broadcast Live Events

Are you celebrating an event in your office?

It could be wishing a staff member a happy birthday. What a great way to show off the friendly culture within your business by filming a staff member getting a birthday cake and being overwhelmed by the office crew singing birthday wishes.

Very cool.

For something more businesslike, why not film an online auction live.

Perhaps you could do a snippet of a marketing meeting occurring on a seller's house live. This could be a 'behind-the-scenes look on how your team markets property; ideal for potential sellers thinking about moving on.

10. **Run a contest**

People love to win things.

Running a contest live usually brings in a large audience.

And when you draw the winner, go Live!

Facebook Live is a great vehicle to generate leads and it's FREE!

STRATEGY #9
Podcast Marketing

Podcasting is <u>the</u> buzzword in 2020. It's been around for awhile but is still relatively new in the real estate world. It's the radio of blogging.

This is a little different in the podcast world though. There are around 650,000 podcast channels on iTunes making it a pretty crowded battlefield.

So, is it worth all the effort to create a regular podcast show and will it generate you leads?

PODCASTING SUPERSTAR

Here are some strategies to improve your chances in winning the podcast challenge.

1. **Lessen the competition, go local**

   Podcasting is churning out its own superstars like the music and film businesses. This would seem to be a daunting prospect of having to compete with these industry God's.

   Real estate has its podcasting rock stars like Tom Ferry, Elite Agent, Tim Neary and Kevin Turner to name a few who are crowding the top spots on the listening charts.

   But there is a way to snap up a listen worthy sector of the podcasting market within the real estate category – go local.

   Instead of trying to dominate the world or even your country (initially at least) why not shoot for your local market listeners and become the source in your local town.

   In a time poor society, people are craving for local insights into the real estate world and your podcast could be the ticket for their listening ears.

2. **Have a clear message**

What will your podcast be about? What is the message you are trying to convey to the listening market in your area?

By being consistent and delivering the same message week in and week out, you'll be the channel people will tune into to hear about the local real estate market.

Your channel will be the place where they can get all the pricing news about housing or apartment selling in their area.

You deliver local insights about planning decisions the government is making.

Interviewing local celebrities could be a nice touch to boost interest and bring in a new audience for your weekly talk show.

3. **Find your super listeners**

What's a super listener? A podcast addict! Somebody who listens to 10+ podcasts per week.

The majority of these people (+50%) click on a podcast and listen immediately. Eighty-one percent of them subscribe to a channel and automatically download podcasts to be listened to at a later date.

Super listeners love to go deep. Make sure you give them plenty of content around certain themes that satisfies their thirst for content.

4. **Have interesting guests**

Having guests on your show gives a different voice other than your own. But when you are just starting out, where do you find these guests?

You can find local identities but how do you find the big 'celebrities'.

Amazon is your answer. It has the best potential guest speakers for your podcast.

Go to the real estate section and check out the top 100 authors.

Podcasting can be done anywhere in the world, so it's easy to connect with a guest outside of your country.

Within the broad real estate niche, there are various sub niches. Real estate sales, buying and investment are just a few.

These sub niches are ideal for uncovering more potential speakers.

5. **Be everywhere your audience is**

Carefully look at the analytics of your channel and be sure you are hanging out on social media platforms where they are.

If your listeners are 25 – 34-year-old Mums, then Instagram is where you need to be.

If you are running a property management podcast helping tenants find great properties in your area, perhaps Snap Chat or Tik-Tok might be your platform.

Post content regularly on those platforms inviting people to check out your podcast.

6. **Get to the top; connect with influencers**

Find out who the influencers are in your niche. Make a direct approach and see if you can get their help.

Most will be looking for a gratuity, so you may have to pay usually via their agent.

7. **External sources can also be helpful.**

Get to know local journalists who write in the real estate space. You might have to shout a few coffees or lunches but their influence by way of nice article in the local newspaper can bring you a lot of attention.

Guest appearances on other podcasting shows can also help you climb the ladder; especially if they are in a real estate genre that's not competing directly with yours.

Podcasting is the new radio and it allows to cast your voice far and wide. Grab a real estate niche, keep it local and you'll soon be hitting the top of the charts.

STRATEGY #10
Buy Online Websites

This not for the faint hearted or the shallow pocket real estate agent, but a fast way to build traffic to your own website is to buy another site in your niche and direct the traffic to your site.

Sounds expensive? It might be but the upside can be huge.

Firstly, you'll need to make the most expensive investment before you can see results. The investment is in your mind and it needs to shift towards this way of thinking.

Buying income producing assets is not completely foreign to real estate agents.

Many will invest in purchasing rent rolls in order to build their asset value while providing an income along the way. This practice has been around for a long time and agents seem comfortable with it.

Sometimes they work and others are a complete disaster especially if the acquisition requires financing. Should the valuation drop against the loan during the time an agent is paying off the purchase, the bank will come knocking.

In some cases, the agent can pacify the bank. Other times they may have to tip some money in to keep the bank happy or if things are too far gone, the bank will insist the asset is sold.

Buying online real estate websites is similar. Entry levels can be cheaper but can creep into the hundreds of thousands of dollars.

If you think this could be a real possibility for you (and your mindset is shifting) read on to discover how you can get a flood of traffic to your website, get more leads and make more money.

BUY HIGH TRAFFIC WEBSITES

Upside of buying an established website

1. **Somebody else has done the heavy lifting**

   All the set-up stuff has been done. The design, layout, page creation and blog articles have been done. You don't get bogged down with menial tasks.

You can now focus on the marketing.

2. **You don't need to be an expert**

Site creation takes a bit of knowledge even if you're outsourcing the process. Getting traffic also takes time. Even poor performing sites get some traffic.

The expertise in product creation has already been done for you when you are buying.

3. **Customer lists come with these sites**

Usually the seller has a list of existing and past customers. This can be very handy for you to continue to nurture and make more sales.

4. **Existing revenue**

By carefully researching sites for sale, you'll discover that some have a decent revenue stream.

This revenue is a key driver in the valuation of the business.

If understanding financial profit and loss sheets is not your strength, send the details to your accountant, business broker or to a site broker.

Firms like EmpireFlippers.com and Flippa.com are reputable for helping you with is.

Finally go with your gut. Start small and tread warily. The biggest benefit in buying a site will be the redirection of traffic to your existing site.

The more traffic the better the opportunity to rank on Google. The higher the ranking the more opportunity you have to capture leads and grow your business.

What type of sites could you buy to get more traffic?

According to Alexa (owned by Amazon) industry traffic comes from various sources.

1. **Search**

   Tax planning and accounting businesses get 62.9% of their traffic directly from people searching that topic. A website around this topic with a bias toward tax planning for property could be a good purchase.

   Travel sites gain 54.9% of their traffic from direct searches. While trying to buy Expedia or Trivago may be out of your budget, what about looking at local sites within your area.

   Accommodation in Mudgee might be a site with some traffic and low cashflow which could be obtained economically.

Food and drink sites get 54% of their traffic from search. A local guide site in your town might be a perfect acquisition.

2. Referral

Traffic referred from another site is a good source.

Real estate sites get about 13.5% of their traffic from referrals. Think of your major real estate portals and that figure would be about right.

If you could acquire a small site, then your traffic should increase.

3. Social

News, weather and information sites get around 12.5% of their traffic from social sites.

You could acquire a local weather site to boost your traffic.

4. Technology

Sites that can offer people and easy way to do something usually attracts a lot of traffic.

Apps around agent commission calculators, comparable market analysis or property investment calculators could be good drivers. Build the apps your self or a site already doing it with existing traffic; the choice is yours.

[[SUCCESS STORY]] Neil Patel – SEO Expert

Neil Patel is a SEO God. He knows how to get traffic to his website.

Occasionally he'll buy sites with good traffic flow. He's been known to have spent $500,000 on acquiring a good traffic site.

And it seems to work.

Today his site gets over 3.6 million views a month!

STRATEGY #11
Pay Per Click Advertising

If you're looking for quick results, you are going to have to pay. Content marketing and SEO strategies might be free (if you write your own articles) but they do take several months to gain traction and produce results.

But if you are prepared to spend some money, you might discover markets not previously reached by you that could be very profitable.

Every venture of course does come with some risks.

By engaging in pay per click advertising (PPC) you are using a medium to display your ads and you pay every time somebody clicks on your ad. That could be expensive if your clicks don't convert to sales.

Let me clear up one thing right now before we go on.

If by reading the previous few lines and your mind went BOOM with the thought of you clicking on a competitor's ad like a drunk with a twitch, then forget it.

Google or any other platform can track your ISP address (that's the one that looks like 193.567.234.913 etc) and you'll get shut down. You don't want that to happen.

Let's just out smart the opposition with better ads instead.

PPC STRATEGY

PPC advertising is expensive; isn't it?

Most advertisers think that this form of advertising is costly as margins are paper thin.

And that's true in part. Create a crappy ad, use the wrong keywords, a bad call to action and a lead capture page that does not work, then you'll pay through the nose.

But done right, you'll be able to target markets normally out of reach to content marketing methods and at a quicker rate.

The best form of PPC advertising is paid search advertising. With this type of advertising you can get to buyers exhibiting high intent to purchase. Programmatic advertisers use this method.

Why you should try PPC

1. **Results can be predicted** (to some extent)

   With content marketing you are in the lap of the Gods to some extent. You can write a great article with the right amount of keywords sprinkled throughout, and it flops for reasons unknown.

   Conversely you write a quick, non-researched article and it goes viral. You just never really know what results you are going to get.

   Google can also be unpredictable. It gets in a mood and changes its algorithm regularly. This may result in what's called a Google slap and you end up losing all your traffic.

   PPC advertising can be more predictable as it's not subject to these hissy fits by Google and your results pretty much come down to your advertising spend.

2. **Inbound marketing is slower**

   Good articles take 6 – 12 months to rank on Google. Yes, I've 'fluked' a few to hit the top ranks within 30 – 60 days but most articles don't start producing results until 6 months.

You can speed up the process by hiring good content article writers (just ask me).

There are plenty of sites where cheap copywriters live. But what I've found that real estate is local and therefore content must have a local voice.

Articles written by a nice gentleman from India maybe cheap but your market is very different to his. Cheap articles will cost you thousands in missed opportunities. Talk to professional writers at EmailEdgar.com

3. **Easy to scale**

Once you get the formula right, you can scale your efforts. That may mean investing more money, but if your advertising is proving to be profitable, scaling won't be an issue.

Scaling content articles can be done but that'll require a lot more articles. Do you have the time to write them? Have you found a reliable copywriter to create your articles?

4. **More time to list and sell real estate**

The whole purpose of this book is to turn your business into a lead generation machine so that you can focus on listing and selling real estate.

That's where the money is for you but having leads coming into your business is vital. You either create them yourself or outsource.

PPC is not only Google

I've referenced Google mostly as being the platform for running PPC campaigns but they are not the exclusive source.

1. **Bing**

   Bing is another search engine but doesn't have the clout of Google.

   It is also a platform where your ad spend should be cheaper. Users on the platform testify that their ad costs are generally 33% cheaper.

   Bing is well set up and it maybe worth experimenting on that platform.

2. **Facebook Ads**

   This is a very solid platform and easy to run ads. Some say it's cheaper than Google but you'll need to get your targeting right for this to occur.

   Facebook ads are a great addition to your content strategy.

Create an eye-catching Facebook post and link back to your blog article.

This drives traffic to your website, creates a strong DA 100 backlink and can convert your article into sales.

3. **LinkedIn**

If you are a business to business real estate firm (commercial real estate) LinkedIn is your playground.

Your viewers to your ads are more professional and they respond well to ads that help them improve their business, network or get a better job.

4. **YouTube Ads**

YouTube is the second biggest search engine next to Google, its parent.

People search YouTube like they do on Google; to get information.

If you create a lot of 'how to' style videos, YouTube can be a very handy traffic driver to your website.

"How to clean your pool for just $5/week"

"Interior painting to sell your home faster"

"Improve your driveway, improve you sale price"

PPC is not a set and forget process

You'll need to monitor your ads regularly. Minor tweaks will be the norm.

Split testing is not an option; it's mandatory. You need to understand which ad performs better. Simple adjustments like the change of a heading or keyword can make a big difference to the performance of an ad.

No matter which platform you use, PPC advertising should be part of your lead generation strategy.

STRATEGY #12
Send Out Cards

When was the last time you got a card in the mail? Your birthday? Christmas?

How did you feel?

If you're like most people, you loved it. The only other piece of direct mail we normally get is either a bill or an advertising brochure shoved into our letterbox; both are not desirable.

So, if the receiving of a card is so pleasurable, why aren't you sending out more cards out yourself to potential customers or existing clients?

Cards are inconvenient and costly are the general responses. And that can be true.

You've got to go to a card shop, select the card, write on it and then address it. This would take you away from your office for at least thirty minutes to an hour.

Not all card shops have a great choice. You could waste another 30 minutes looking through all the cards or worse still you may need to visit other card shops.

The whole process can be very time consuming, even if you get your assistant to do the selection for you.

Cost of cards are not cheap either. A typical branded card will set you back $5 - $7. That's ok if you are giving it to somebody special but if you were using cards as a prospecting tool, then your outlay may run into the tens of thousands.

Selecting the card is only part of the battle though. We've already determined that it could be time consuming and costly, but then you need to post it.

That requires a visit to the post office. If you live in Australia, you'll know what it's like using Australia Post facilities.

They are under staffed and processing of your request takes ages.

Crikey you just want to buy a stamp! Meanwhile the que is ten people long and is being held up by an 'Aunt Marg" lady at the head of the que trying to pay her electricity and gas bill and repeatedly hits the wrong button on the credit card processing machine causing even more delays.

What amazes me though that while the postal service acknowledges their service is sub-par they have not hesitation in racking up the prices on a regular basis.

Australian stamps start from $1; this can be costly on a mass mailout!

The email version of a card is no substitute though.

Because of this calamity, most real estate agents have abandoned sending out real cards. Instead that have adopted sending cards via email.

I couldn't think of a more tacky, impersonal act. I delete all cards via email and unsubscribe from the sender.

Sending a card is a relationship building tool not a last-minute gesture sent as bulk email spam.

THE BEST CARD SENDING SYSTEM (WITHOUT LEAVING HOME)

There is a way to send real cards without you leaving home. You can choose from 10,000+ card templates or create your own. The card can even be printed in your own hand writing.

Send Out Cards is a technology company that gives you the ability to send a physical, printable stamped card, to a recipient directly from your computer without visiting a card shop or standing in line to buy stamps.

The whole process can be completed with just one click from your home or office at a fraction of the cost of a branded card.

Check out the process with one of the leaders in Send Out Cards. **Deb Mullen** (Google her, see her LinkedIn, Facebook) will allow you to test drive the system by sending a card for free.

Get her to show you how the system can create campaigns for you that will not only build relationships, create more leads but deliver more sales. She's helped hundreds of real estate agents and she'll help you become an elite agent in your area too.

STRATEGY #13
YouTube Marketing

Video is so hot now. It has been for a while but during COVID-19 times, it's really taken off.

In this section I'm not going to talk about layouts, covers, thumbnails or basic design. They are important though. If you want to have a professionally looking **YouTube Channel grab my free guide here** Content Charlie YouTube Channel Checklist (https://dl.bookfunnel.com/y61bh3isl6).

Instead I'm going to outline the necessary ingredients to have a great channel.

1. **Regular content**

   In order to keep your subscribers coming back to your channel and building relationships you'll need to upload videos regularly.

   When starting out and growing your audience, upload short videos of around two minutes. This way you can tackle a big topic over several smaller videos.

2. Create a catchy headline

I've been banging on about this throughout this book. Headlines are critical if you want somebody to click onto your video – and that's the name of the game.

Take a look at your news channels. Look at the headlines they use to grab your attention for an upcoming show.

"Governor declares war on breast feeding mums"

It's sensationalizing at its best but it works. Some would say it's click baiting and they'd be partially right.

But the main aim of a heading is to get a viewer to watch the video. Nothing else. If your headline is vanilla and dull, they'll move on.

"Real estate agent shoots home owner in her pool". Let's hope he used film!

3. Thumbnails

I said I wasn't going to discuss channel design but I couldn't resist slamming this one again because it's so critical.

To give uniformity, clear lines and making your videos pop, create a thumbnail for each video.

No more cover images with your moth wide open or your eyes half closed. Thumbnails eliminate that.

To be able to use custom thumbnails you will have to verify your channel. It's easy but you'll need to have a gmail account.

Grab the checklist previously for more details.

4. **Add your logo**

This gives you more brand awareness.

You can use watermarks to protect your videos as well.

5. **Promote via other channels**

Reach out to other channels and ask if they'll share your content.

They'll be happy to if you give them a shout out in your video.

Look for competitors who are doing well; the ones that have more subscribers and views. Add or improve upon their content or upload a video that comments on one of their videos.

"Gary Vee says you shouldn't own a home. I disagree"

6. **Have great descriptions**

I mentioned the importance of headlines earlier. Your description is just as important. If its boring, nobody will watch you your video.

Your description should be at least one paragraph long. It must include a sprinkling of your main keyword.

If you don't want to write out a description, get your video transcribed.

Rev.com will do this for you for $1/minute. Simply send them your video and you'll have the description back within the hour usually.

7. **Tags**

Keywords that describe your video. They are necessary to find your video. Use a keyword tool planner like Ubersuggest to find relevant keywords for your video.

8. **Ask for likes, comments and shares**

YouTube loves videos that have likes, comments and shares. They promote these videos higher within their search function because viewers have already given their approval.

When you are shooting a video say something like "If you like this video please give it the thumbs up by liking, commenting and sharing it"

And don't forget to ask them to subscribe; usually at the beginning

"If this is your first time to my channel, I invite you to hit the Subscribe button and hit the bell. That way you'll be notified every time I upload a new video"

9. **Let people know when you upload**

Good YouTube channel owners let their viewers know when they upload videos.

Be consistent and pick a time each week you'll upload your videos.

Announce it on your YouTube cover – 'New videos every Tuesday and Thursday'

STRATEGY #14
HR Departments

Do you have any large companies, institutions or government bodies in your area?

Most of these entities will have a HR department who look after staff interests and in some cases assisting them with settling into a new area.

Hospitals

Hospitals for example employ thousands of doctors and nurses. Many of these professionals come from outside the local area and they rely on the expertise of their employer to guide them in finding suitable accommodation in the area.

Establish contact with the HR department and build a relationship with key personal by letting them know the services you provide as a real estate agent.

Perhaps you could offer a 'special' package for personnel who use your services eg discount commission, rental rebate, utility connection service.

Also don't forget the referrer by rewarding them on a regular basis as well. While the HR staff maybe reluctant to accept cash rewards, most would appreciate a shopping voucher or a restaurant voucher in your area or a donation to the hospital.

Universities

Just like hospitals, Universities have a lot of moving staff.

Out of town lecturers need assistance in finding good accommodation.

Schools

Schools can offer a similar opportunity but have an additional one as well.

Why not approach the HR department, school admin or the Principal and offer a service to speak to graduating school kids about renting their first home?

Give them a checklist of what to look for in renting a property, their rights and what they'll need to make their application proceed smoothly.

Back this up with a free giveaway pack and your name will be top of mind when they want to rent a property.

You could even become top of mind if their parents are buying or selling a home.

STRATEGY #15
Instagram Marketing

With around 800 million monthly users on Instagram, it's a social media platform you should be on, particularly if your real estate business sells or leases to a younger demographic.

The site attracts a lot of influencers and with the right plan, you to could have a booming business generating you a ton of leads.

In this chapter I'm going to discuss what is necessary to create a good Instagram profile, the type of account you'll need and some strategies to attract the right audience and grow your business.

INSTAGRAM STRATEGY

Let's start with the right account.

Is real estate a good niche on Instagram?

The most popular accounts on Instagram center around fashion, beauty, food and travel.

Real estate can also be a great niche if you adopt a 'beauty' aspect or a 'how to' option.

Beautiful luxurious homes are appealing, as are images showing us how to do things. How to renovate a bathroom, how to landscape your garden or topics or something similar.

Grab a business account

Many of you probably started your Instagram journey with a personal account, and that's great.

But if you really want to extract the juice out of Instagram and open up the whole enchilada of features you'll need to convert your account to a business account.

Just click on your settings and 'switch to business account' and you'll be set to go.

Have a business strategy

Let's face it there's a ton of material being posted to social media willy nilly.

That means it's becoming more difficult to grab somebody's attention. You have to be above average; more likely you'll need to be amazing!

But even then, it'll be hard to get in front of people.

You'll need to be amazing AND different.

People don't just follow brands. They follow people. Followers are interested in seeing what Roger Federer is up to over looking at Nike.

Share your opinion

People are drawn to a message. They are interested in hearing your opinion PROVIDED is delivering value to them. Nobody is drawn to a rant of egotistical garbage.

So, if you can deliver your point of view as to why a salt water pool has considerably more upside than a freshwater pool, can save the user money and have low maintenance costs, then an audience will listen to your message over and over.

Why you do what you do

Let people know why you are in real estate not what you do. Talk about your mission statement and show how that gets you up every day; selling real estate is only a buy product.

Apple is the best exponent of this. They slam Samsung.

Both sell computers and phones but Apply lets you know they are different. How they do this is that they engage with their audience about their mission and they just so happen to sell computers and phones.

Read Simon Sinek's Start With Why – it's brilliant!

Use hashtags for a wider audience

Hashtags have been used effectively on Twitter gaining a user 21% more reach by including two hashtags in their posts. But over two hashtags, surprising there is a drop in engagement. Message here is not to overdo it.

Google the best hashtags for real estate and you'll be swamped. Sprinkle two of these into your posts to grow your audience.

Here's the top 5 hashtags on Instagram:

- Love 942,781,659 posts
- Instagood 506,823,755 posts
- Photoooftheday 365,234,815 posts
- Tbt 352,409,612 posts
- Cute 299,830,337 posts

Location hashtags are also popular. If your brand has a mascot, like L J Hooker's bear, upload the 'Thank you Mr. Hooker' bear at the Grand Canyon, dinner on Darling Harbour with a view of the Opera House or anything else that may grab your audience's attention.

And finally, if a hashtag post is performing well, repost it later on. You entire feed didn't see the original post, so don't worry about doubling up.

Comment on good posts

This is something you should be doing on a regular basis, both your other content and yours.

It's easier said than done because consistency is hard but is necessary if you want to crack the social media code.

Jump into your Insights and see how much engagement and reach you are getting on each post. You'll find that reach and comments go hand in hand.

So, ensure your top posts have sufficient comments including comments from you. Never not answer comments either. Make the person who posted a comment feel important by you acknowledging them with a response.

When posting yourself, start the ball rolling by adding a comment. It'll encourage others to express their views.

Share other people's content

It's time consuming to come up with great images all by yourself.

Why not approach a local bathroom specialist and use their images to engage more views? Hopefully the bathroom company may do the same exposing your real estate brand to their customers.

Create a contest

Photo contests do really well on Instagram. People love to get involved especially if their photo is exhibited and a prize is given to the winner.

And the photos don't have to be amazingly outstanding showing positive images.

What about a contest around the worst homes occupied by hoarders? Contrast those with after pictures once you've had a clean up company come in and declutter the premises.

You could work the project as a joint venture with the cleaning company, sharing costs, and both marketing the project to your respective audiences.

Emojis make people smile

They grab attention and generally make people feel good. Add them to your content

STRATEGY #16
Facebook Paid Marketing

We've looked at getting organic traffic on Facebook in the hope that this might lead to getting leads.

But with organic reach dipping to around 1-2% on your newsfeed, it's very difficult to do business organically.

I'm still a big fan of Facebook Live and building brand by omnipresence (with an occasional paid boost), but when it comes to driving real eyeballs to your Facebook page, you are going to need to pay for them.

And to be honest, that's exactly what Mr. Zuckerberg wants; paid advertising.

In this chapter I'm going to focus on a few main things that will get you results. I'm assuming you've already run some ads and possibly not profitably.

So, the basic set up of ads and using your Ads Manager will be mostly glossed over. If you need to

learn how to set up your account, Google Facebook ad
set up and you'll be swamped for choice.

FACEBOOK PAID ADVERTISING

Let's get started.

1. **Have a strategy and design your Facebook Ad
   funnel**

   A Facebook ad funnel is a strategy that moves
   freezing cold traffic to warm leads ready to buy
   over a number of campaigns. The funnel can be
   broken down into 3 basic sections:

   ### Awareness

   Since you are dealing with cold traffic (people
   who do not know you), you'll need to create
   awareness for your business. It establishes you as
   an authority and creates more engagement in
   your newsfeed.

   ### Engagement

   In this section you are introducing your products
   or services by directing people back to your
   website. Whether you have lifestyle acreage
   properties to sell or you offer auction services, it is
   the engagement section where this begins.

Website marketing

Drive sales from your website.

Depending where you are at in your marketing, will depend on what type of funnel marketing you need to do. It may mean that you only need to do two of the above promotions. If however you are starting from scratch you'll need all three.

2. **Install your Facebook pixel**

Running your Facebook ads is great but which ones are working and which ones do you need to fix or delete.

You'll need to install a Facebook pixel on your website to track your results. This requires getting a piece of code and placing it on your website. Not too difficult but if you need help jump onto YouTube and search Facebook pixel installation'.

Another thing you'll need to track are your conversions. This is referred to as either conversion events or standard events. YouTube videos can help you with the set up.

If you would prefer somebody to actually do the work for you, visit Upworks.com or Fiverr.com and search for the service you need help with.

Rates on both these sites are reasonable; Fiverr is generally cheaper for most things though.

3. Target audiences

Audiences on Facebook fall into three main areas – cold, warm and hot.

<u>Cold audiences</u> are the most distant group but also the largest. They are the audience that most business comes from once you've built up your awareness and engagement. So don't dismiss them.

<u>Warm audiences</u> are those who are aware of you and engaged a little.

<u>Hot audiences</u> have visited your website, checked out your products or service and possibly have bought. They form the foundation for your custom and lookalike audiences.

4. Create custom or lookalike audiences

As the name suggests, a lookalike audience looks like one of your existing audiences.

To create your first lookalike audience you'll need to create a custom audience. These are usually from people who have visited your Facebook page within a specific time frame.

The most common tome frame is 180 days but Facebook does allow you to build custom audiences around 90, 60, 30, 20 or 10 days. The success of these custom audiences comes down to the size of the audiences collected.

Initially this would mean that probably you'll only get a decent list from your 180 day list but as you continue to market and audiences rush to your page, the remaining time frames will also grow into a decent pool.

Facebook has the biggest engaged audience of all the social media platforms.

It would be crazy to ignore it but with organic reach on your newsfeed, you will have to use paid advertising.

There is no entry exam to start advertising which can cause a lot of newbies to over spend and blow their money quickly. They also drive up the costs of ads for which Facebook is becoming dearer every year.

For you to keep your costs down follow the four steps above.

They'll make your ads more effective, help you build awareness and engagement, turn cold traffic into warm or hot, and generate leads that will make sale for you.

STRATEGY # 17
Programmatic Marketing

Programmatic marketing is the buzzword of the day but not many real estate agents know about it and therefore don't use it.

Of all retail display ads in the US, 80% of them use programmatic marketing.

So, what is it and how can real estate agents use it to generate leads and make more sales?

Briefly, programmatic marketing is a way to automatically buy and optimize digital campaigns using machine learning and artificial intelligence.

Ads are created via real time auctions as visitors hop onto a site.

PROGRAMMATIC MARKETING DEFINED

The use of Artificial Intelligence and machine learning to buy advertising in real-time, instead of going through human negotiations and pre-set prices (Source: Match2One).

How are the ads targeted?

If you want better accuracy your ads need to be targeted towards an audience

- **Contextual ads**

  Ads are based on the context of a website. For a fashion brand, their ads should be shown on sites around fashion eg Prada, Vogue magazine.

  Real estate agencies in Australia my want their ads appearing on portals like REA or Domain.

  In the US, agents would parget their bidding toward appearing on Realtor.com or Trulia or Zillow.

  In the UK, real estate portals like Rightmove and On The Market would be the best options for UK real estate agents

- **Keyword targeting**

  You might want to appear on sites where articles appear about real estate keywords and phrases.

  Let's say you are an apartment selling specialist. Keywords like buying an apartment, selling and apartment, living in an apartment, apartment costs or the benefits of apartment living may be a great place for you to display a programmatic ad about yourself where these keywords appear.

You can also include negative keywords contained in articles on your own website because you don't want to pay for impressions for an asset that's already producing traffic for you.

- **Geo-targeting**

  Display ads based on location. If you are marketing a property in Melbourne, it would be inefficient use of your advertising spend to be directed to residents in Biloela (2,500 miles away).

- **Retargeting**

  You generally only get 2% of visitors to buy something the first time.

  Retargeting is important to bring the other 98% back to your product.

How much does programmatic advertising cost?

That's difficult to determine as you'll need to engage a media buying agency to place the ads for you.

You can Google programmatic marketing agencies to begin your research.

Australian real estate network, First National Real estate is the only group that has an in-house media company conducting such a service for its agents. Costs are around $250 for 40,000 impressions delivered over a 30-day period.

REA also runs their audience maximizer program in Australia for about $600 for 25,000 impressions.

The benefits of programmatic marketing

Programmatic ads use AI thereby making them laser targeted and great bang for buck.

Ads get seen by the right people which gives a higher chance of a sale being made.

These ads also deliver huge traffic back to a website thereby pushing it up in the Google rankings. If your selling a property with programmatic marketing, you'll experience better positioning on Google and an increase in your organic traffic.

And of course, you have a great opportunity to sell more real estate.

[[SUCCESS STORY]] – First National Tamborine

Set on top of Tamborine Mountain in the Gold Coast hinterland, this family run business has successfully endured a lot of competition from other real estate agencies and survived.

However, visibility on Google was a problem. They weren't on page one for the mountain and that meant business was sliding.

They adopted programmatic marketing and saw their website traffic increase by 417% and they returned to the front page on Google, hitting the #1 spot for Tamborine real estate agents.

Sales are up, property managements are growing and this business is once again dominating the mountain.

ABOUT THE AUTHOR

Who am I?

Hi, I am Greg Reed and I'm an ex real estate selling agent, email copywriter and content creation marketer for businesses hell bent on growth.

What can I do for you?

I write words that sell using email copywriting, engaging social media or highly converting blog articles so you can focus on listing, selling and leasing real estate.

Why Listen to Me?

I'm an advisor and contributor to some really cool companies

- **First National Real Estate** - advised up to 80+ real estate offices yearly over 13 years about growing their business with a strong focus on lead generation.
- **Magnetic Real Estate Agent** – a real estate blog with 25,000+ visitors monthly

- **Juggernaut India** – webinar content creator and speaker on building a writing business.
- **Wealthy Writer Group** – part of the No Pants Project – case study interviewee.
- **C T Mitchell Books** – content creator, email copywriter for this 13 x #1 Amazon bestselling author.
- **Ben Settle LLC** – student of the Daily Email.
- **Dan Kennedy** – student of the world's #1 direct sales marketer.
- **Neville Medhora** – student of the Kopywriting Kourse.
- **Michael Shreeve** – copywriter to Mel Robbins, Brendan Burchard – student

Some Nice Things Said About Greg Reed

David Forrest, FN Cairns Central: Greg has tremendous knowledge when it comes to writing and social media. Couple that with his skills gained in sales, particularly real estate and you will understand why I have learnt so much from him. He has helped us understand the digital world and the need for content. He made one suggestion to our website and overnight we went back to page one in the Google search, and he has been coaching us with our blogs ever since.

Jamie Buttigieg, StoryBrand AU: Greg is a talented marketer who truly understands buyer behaviour. He can take your existing database and breathe new life (and sales) into it. If you are not using email marketing, you are potentially missing out on a massive source of sales and leads.... the best part, Greg can automate your processes to reduce your effort and maximise your returns!

Debbie Fletcher, National Property Manager: Greg Reed's knowledge of real estate and running a successful business has been extremely valuable to many First National members. His expertise on how to successfully use social media for business exposure is second to none.

Anthony Bowers, Tallant Asia: Greg Reed is a top professional who is dedicated to achieving excellent results for his clients and partners. His wealth of experience and strategic vision allow him to seek out and find innovative ways of doing things that benefits all concerned. If you are looking to enhance your networking, social media presence and indeed looking to refine and improve your overall business process model, then I can highly recommend Greg

Come Join Me at <u>EmailEdgar.com</u>

I'd love for you to join me on my email list. Here's what to expect:

- **2 emails per week.** They are full of new real estate marketing techniques.
- **Unsubscribe anytime.** If you hate my writing, just click one button and *poof* I'm gone from your life forever!
- **The first email is amazing.** It contains free bonus stuff (another book).

Need Done-For-You Services?

I can write your next blog article or email marketing campaign. Just visit Email Edgar.com and Contact me or Book A Call. Spend your time selling!

WHO WANTS TO BE A LEAD GENERATION JEDI?

From the outset of this book I made it clear that operating a successful real estate business required you to become a real estate lead generating jedi.

It's pretty simple to do but not necessarily easy. What is easy to do is also easy not to do. Anybody can succeed at becoming a lead generating machine but not everybody will.

The difference lies in your focus to apply the tasks at hand to generate more leads and for you to take action. Way back in the dim dark ages of the '90's I told you of one of my greatest days in real estate sales when I sold 11 homes in just 5 hours.

I too could have been like my colleagues and hoped things were going to happen for me. I could have relaxed by the television every night watching some mind-numbing show and thinking buyers were going to rush into my office the next day and buy their new dream home.

Instead I adopted this type of plan to generate my real estate leads

- Create a personal plan and focus on achieving it
- Blocked out time to generate leads – daily, weekly
- Be accountable for my lead generation activities
- Create a supportive environment both at work and at home
- Kept my energy up to stay the course

As a result, I sold 11 homes in 5 hours; most of my colleagues sold none! And I've had multiple 12 – 16 sale months since.

The 17 strategies mentioned are not conclusive. They are merely a start. There are literarily thousands of ideas out there for you to implement. But if you want to become a millionaire selling agent, you must become a lead generating master.

Thanks for reading this book. Adopt what you like and discard the rest. If you liked this book, I'd love a positive review on Amazon.

I wish you every success in your real estate career.

Greg Reed

www.ingramcontent.com/pod-product-compliance
Lightning Source LLC
Chambersburg PA
CBHW031900200326
41597CB00012B/491